Twelve Hats for Lena

To Lena and to her dad, Gary, who wears many hats

Margaret K. McElderry Books
An imprint of Simon & Schuster Children's Publishing Division
1230 Avenue of the Americas
New York, NY 10020

Book design by Daniel Roode
The text of this book is set in Bernhard Modern.
The illustrations are rendered in collage, gouache, and colored pencils.
Printed in Hong Kong
2 4 6 8 10 9 7 5 3 1
Library of Congress Cataloging-in-Publication Data
Katz, Karen.
Twelve hats for Lena : a book of months / Karen Katz.— 1st ed.
p. cm.
Summary: Lena Katz creates hats appropriate for each month of the year.
ISBN 0-689-84873-0
[1. Hats—Fiction. 2. Months—Fiction. 3. Year—Fiction. 4. Stories in rhyme.] I. Title.
PZ8.3.K1283 Tw 2002
[E]—dc21
2001044907

FIRST
EDITION

Twelve Hats for Lena

A Book of Months

♥

Karen Katz

Margaret K. McElderry Books

New York London Toronto Sydney Singapore

a b c d e f g h i j k l m n o p

Lena Katz is making some hats—
one for each month of the year.
She imagines what makes each month so great
and begins to paste and decorate.

January

starts the year with snow.

February

is the time to give hearts with bows.

March

winds swirl and we hear robins sing.

April

is the month we hide eggs
and see the first signs of spring.

May

seedlings grow into flower bouquets.

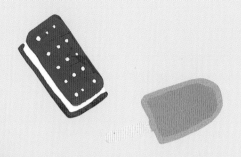

June

23rd is Lena's birthday!

July

is bright with sparklers
and boats with big sails.

August

is the month to collect sand in our pails.

September

is the summer's end.
We go back to school
and meet new friends.

October

is the month for spooky cats,
ghosts, and treats, and funny hats.

November

leaves begin to fall. Families gather
to give thanks to all.

December

is a month with much to celebrate.
But how will Lena choose to decorate?

Three dreidels for Hanukkah tucked in the trim?

Or some fruit for Kwanzaa placed on the brim?

A big fir tree with lights so bright
might be fine to celebrate Christmas night.

Lena knows just what to do.

She pastes
      and sews
          and cuts
             and glues.

And when the hat is finally done,
it is . . .

HOW TO MAKE LOTS OF HATS FROM ONE SIMPLE PATTERN

1. On a large piece of poster board trace around a big soup-pot lid to draw a big circle. Have an adult help you cut it out. This will be the brim of your hat.

2. Measure the diameter of your head by wrapping a one-inch-wide strip of paper around it, right above your ears. Tape the paper strip together to make a circle where the ends overlap.

3. Place the circular head-measurement strip in the middle of your poster-board brim and trace around it with a pencil. Have an adult help you cut out the hole from the brim.

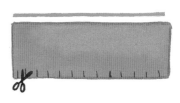

4. Undo the tape on the head-measurement strip and lay it flat on a rectangular piece of poster board. Have an adult help you cut a strip of poster board one inch longer than the head-measurement strip and as tall as you want your hat to be. Form tabs by making one-inch-deep cuts two inches apart all along the bottom edge of the poster board.

5. Roll the poster-board strip to make a cylinder that will fit snugly inside the brim of your hat. Use tape or ask an adult to help you use a stapler to hold the cylinder together.

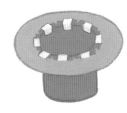

6. Fit the cylinder, tabs-side down, into the brim. Fold the tabs back and tape the tabs to the underside of the brim.

7. Have an adult help you cut out a circle of poster board that measures one inch wider than the top of the cylinder. Form tabs by making one-inch-deep cuts two inches apart all around the circle. Place the circle on the top of the cylinder and fold the tabs down into the top of the cylinder. Tape the tabs inside the cylinder. Your top hat is finished!

HERE ARE SOME OTHER HATS YOU CAN MAKE FROM THE BASIC DESIGN

Instead of making a cylinder for the body of your hat, roll the poster board and tape it, so it is shaped like a cone.

Have an adult help you staple a plastic bowl upside down onto the top of the brim.

Make a cone, cut tabs along the bottom, and tape it into the brim.

Glue a winter cap onto the brim.

Have an adult help you cut shapes in the top of the cylindrical hat to make a crown.

. . . a holiday hat for everyone!